Erica Jong

AT THE EDGE OF THE BODY

GRANADA
London Toronto Sydney New York

Granada Publishing Limited
Frogmore, St Albans, Herts AL2 2NF
and
36 Golden Square, London W1R 4AH
866 United Nations Plaza, New York, NY 10017, USA
117 York Street, Sydney, NSW 2000, Australia
100 Skyway Avenue, Rexdale, Ontario M9W 3A6, Canada
61 Beach Road, Auckland, New Zealand

Published by Granada Publishing 1981

ISBN 0 246 11518 1 (hardback)
ISBN 0 586 05395 6 (paperback)

Printed and bound in Great Britain by
Cox & Wyman Ltd, Reading

Granada ®
Granada Publishing ®

Erica Jong is that rarest of all literary combinations – a real poet who is also a best-selling novelist. Her first book of poems, *Fruits & Vegetables*, established her as one of the new breed of women writers. Her second, *Half-Lives*, showed a darkening and maturing vision and a flair for satire. A third volume, *Loveroot*, contained, among other poetic subjects, tributes to Keats, Colette, Whitman and other writers from whom she learnt her trade. Poems from these three books have appeared in two previous Granada Paperbacks which are now available: Erica Jong's *Selected Poems* and *Selected Poems II*.

Her first novel, *Fear of Flying*, began its long life as a *succès d'estime*, a *succès de scandale*, a world-wide bestseller and eventually a modern classic. Her second novel, *How to Save Your Own Life*, also became an international bestseller and introduced a new level of candour to contemporary fiction. This was followed in 1980 by her astonishing nineteenth-century historical novel, *Fanny*, hailed as a literary triumph as well as an erotic masterpiece.

It is safe to say that no contemporary writer has been as much discussed, debated, praised, lambasted and *read*. *Fear of Flying* was one of the ten largest selling books of the 1970s, with six million copies in print in the United States alone. Her poetry has been translated almost as widely as her novels.

A native of New York City, Erica Jong now lives in Connecticut with her writer husband, Jonathan Fast, and her young daughter, Molly.

By the same author

For Martha Friedman

Disaster is the avenue
of fortune; and fortune
is the concealment for
disaster.

–LAO-TSE

To succeed is always to fail.
Arrival is death and travelling
is eternal . . .

–J. KRISHNAMURTI

We read the world
wrong and say that
it deceives us.
–RABINDRANATH TAGORE

Contents

I

THE BUDDHA IN THE WOMB

It is for the artist to
proclaim his faith in the
Everlasting Yes.
–RABINDRANATH TAGORE

To write poetry: you have
to be prepared to die.
–THEODORE ROETHKE

If Death

Muse-touched today
I thought how strange
if death should take me
here, now, with half my honours
on, with half my years, unchilded,
loved, well loved, & half
believing in a god of love,
as I did not before, oh say,
half my life ago.

I would give up in peace.
I would go quietly
& not protest my youth
(which anyway tarnishes daily), nor my gift
(which anyway iş only
a way of saying: thank you, life,
hello death);
& not protest my rank
unreadiness.

I am ready. Whenever
the branch breaks,
whenever the film slips
in the sprockets, whenever the light
hisses & burns out, whenever

the lightning strikes, or the ice
slithers me across
into the oncoming traffic lane,
headlights blaring like
the head of God,
or a trumpet blast
of exploding starlight.
Neither the sun nor death
can be looked at steadily
said La Rochefoucauld—
who did not believe much
in love. But I will stare him
down.

At the Edge of
the Body

At the edge of the body
there is said to be
a flaming halo—
yellow, red, blue
or pure white,
taking its colour
from the state
of the soul.

Cynics scoff;
scientists make graphs
to refute it;
editorial writers,
journalists, & even
certain poets,
claim it is only mirage,
trumped-up finery,
illusory feathers,
spiritual shenanigans,
humbug.

But in dreams
we see it,
& sometimes even waking . . .
If the spirit is a bride

about to be married to God,
this is her veil.

Do I believe it?
Do I squint
& regard the perimeter
of my lover's body,
searching for some sign
that his soul
is about to ignite
the sky?

Without squinting,
I almost see it.
An angry red aura
changing to white,
the colour of peace.

I gaze at the place
where he turns into air
& the flames of his skin
combine
with the flames of the sky,
proving
the existence
of both.

Self-Portrait in Shoulder Stand

Old bag of bones
upside down,
what are you searching for
in poetry,
in meditation?

The mother you never had?

The child in you
that you did not conceive?

Death?

Ease from the fear of death?

Revelation?

Dwelling in the house of clouds
where you imagine
you once lived?

'Born alone,
we depart alone.'
Someone said that
during meditation
& I nearly wept.

Oh melancholy lady
behind your clown face,
behind your wisecracks—
how heady it is
to let the ideas rush to your brain!

But even upside down,
you are sad.

Even upside down,
you think of your death.
Even upside down,
you curse the emptiness.

Meditating
on the immobile lotus,
your mind takes flight
like a butterfly
& dabbles in blood-red poppies
& purple heather.

Defying gravity,
defying death,
what makes you think
the body's riddle
is better solved
upside down?

Blood rushes to your head
like images that come too fast
to write.

After a life held in the double grip
of gravity & time,

after a headfirst birth
out of your mother's bowels
& into the earth,
you practise for the next.

You make your body light
so that in time,
feetfirst,
you will be born
into the sky.

My Death

'Death is our eternal companion,'
don Juan said with a most serious
air. 'It is always to our left, at an
arm's length . . . It has always been
watching you. It always will until
the day it taps you.'
                    –CARLOS CASTANEDA

My death
looks exactly like me.
She lives to my left,
at exactly an arm's length.
She has my face, hair, hands;
she ages
as I grow older.

Sometimes, at night,
my death awakens me
or else appears in dreams
I did not write.
Sometimes a sudden wind
blows from nowhere,
& I look left
& see my death.

Alive, I write
with my right hand only.
When I am dead,
I shall write with my left.

But later I will have to write
through others.
I may appear
to future poets
as their deaths.

Zen & the Art of Poetry

Letting the mind go,
letting the pen, the breath,
the movement of images in & out
of the mouth
go calm, go rhythmic
as the rise & fall of waves,
as one sits in the lotus position
over the world,
holding the pen so lightly
that it scarcely stains the page,
holding the breath
in the glowing cage of the ribs,
until the heart
is only a living lantern
fuelled by breath,
& the pen writes
what the heart wills
& the whole world goes out,
goes black,
but for the hard, clear stars
below.

Flame Dance

Black men in flame-coloured
robes somersaulting through
the air, the air itself
bright orange flame
tapering off to blue,
the men's glossy foreheads tinged
with blue, blue highlights
on their glistening ebony skins,
blue notes in their syncopated steps,
the wail of blues on oranges.

Who are they? Why do they come
dancing behind my lids
before sleep? My eyelids
the transparent gauzy scrims
of veiled stages where many dancers
whirl, propelled by a divine choreographer,
& not knowing why they dance,
or why
      I watch.

Tempering

'Because the idea of death is the only thing
that tempers our spirit.'

–DON JUAN TO CARLOS CASTANEDA

Power, passion, despair—
how do we find the strength
to live,
when living
is always nearly impossible
& the poems of the soil strike rock
& the nail in the wall
bends itself
on an iron beam?

Rust, earth, sheared steel,
nails bending back towards their hammerers,
iron returning to red ore,
poets loading their rifts
with passion, despair,
the power that comes from death.

It alone
keeps us strong.
It alone
is a mulch garden ·
strewn with straw
against the weeds,
nurtured by a philosophical farmer
who loves music,

reads the Torah
& studies
the long history
of death.

The Xylophone of the Spine

The cosmos has played
on the xylophone
of my spine,
hitting each vertebra
with a single clear-pitched tone,
making my backbone
reverberate
with the fleshly echo
of the music
of the spheres.

When the flesh falls from these bones,
the notes will be clearer.
When the skin withers
& the spirit sails out
clear as the autumn air,
crisp as the falling leaves,
shining as the waters of our planet
seen from afar
by creatures who are made
of melody,
& who are invisible,
untouchable & far
except when they come to earth
to make music
on our fragile bones.

Is Life the Incurable Disease?

Is life the incurable disease?
The infant is born howling
& we laugh,
the dead man smiles
& we cry,
resisting the passage,
always resisting the passage,
that turns life
into eternity.

Blake sang alleluias
on his deathbed.
My own grandmother,
hardly a poet at all,
smiled
as we'd never seen her smile
before.
Perhaps the dress of flesh
is no more than a familiar garment
that grows looser as one diets
on death, & perhaps we discard it
or give it to the poor in spirit,
who have not learned yet
what blessing it is
to go naked?

Aura

I sit in the black leather chair
meditating
on the plume of smoke that rises
in the air,
riffling the pages of my life
as if it were a book of poems,
flipping through
past & future.

If I go back, back, back,
riding the plume of smoke,
I find I died
in childbirth in another life,
died by fire in the life before that,
died by water twice, or more.

I pick out days
& relive them
as if I were trying on dresses.

When the future beckons,
I follow,
riding another plume of smoke,
feeling the barrier
between skin & air

evaporate,
& my body disappear
like the myth it is.
My cheeks burn against the air,
flaming where two elements collide
& intermingle
becoming one.

Oh explosion at the body's edge!
I live on a ledge of time,
gazing
at the infinite.

The Keys

Broken ivories
playing
the blue piano
of the sea . . .

We have come
from the bitter city
to heal ourselves.
We have come
looking for a patch of beach
not yet built into a fortress
of real-estate greed,
a coral reef
not yet picked clean
of buried treasure,
not yet bare of birds.

The first night in the Keys,
I dreamed I was a bird
soaring over a hilly city,
soaring & dipping
like a gull or egret,
& I thought:
'Ah—this is a flying dream!
Enjoy it.'

But I really think
that my soul
had been transported
for a night
into the body of
a bird
& I was *flying*.

I woke up
exhausted,
arms weary,
eyes red.
The beach was dazzling
with its white sand,
the sun blinding,
& I seemed to know the palm trees
from above
as well as below.

They root in the sand
with elephant feet,
yet they also root
their delicate fronds
in air.
& these are a comfort
as you fly
half bird, half human
through a dream of sky.

Everything was new
to a spirit
so divided
between two kingdoms.
The water was alive

with fishes,
the air with birds
& palm fronds,
clouds, thunderous presences
of rain
gathering & parting,
& fiery sun playing through.

I knew
that I stood
on a patch of earth
connected to the sky,
that my heart beat
with the sea,
that my arms moved
with the clouds,
that my flesh
was finally irrelevant
though it surrounded me
as the case of a piano
surrounds its strings
while the fingers play
on the ivory keys
& the human music
rises to the sky.

The Buddha in the Womb

Bobbing in the waters of the womb,
little godhead, ten toes, ten fingers
& infinite hope,
sails upside down through the world.

My bones, I know, are only a cage
for death.
Meditating, I can see my skull,
a death's head,
lit from within
by candles
which are possibly the suns
of other galaxies.

I know that death
is a movement towards light,
a happy dream
from which you are loath to awaken,
a lover left
in a country
to which you have no visa,
& I know that the horses of the spirit
are galloping, galloping, galloping
out of time
& into the moment called NOW.

Why then do I care
for this upside-down Buddha
bobbling through the world,
his toes, his fingers
alive with blood
that will only sing & die?

There is a light in my skull
& a light in his.
We meditate on our bones only
to let them blow away
with fewer regrets.

Flesh is merely a lesson.
We learn it
& pass on.

II

WITHOUT PARACHUTES

I slept with Yes
but woke to No.
—THEODORE ROETHKE

My dreams don't
understand me.
—THEODORE ROETHKE

The Poetry Suit

I put on my poetry suit.
The prose falls away
like a dream I cannot remember,
the images unravelling like threads
in a cheap dress, sewn in Hong Kong
to feed the hungry mouths
of sweet-faced Chinese children.

Now I am in my poetry suit.
I zip myself into it,
pink as flesh, tight as the suit
I was born in, & looking
seamless as a perfect poem,
gleaming as the golden fleece,
slim as a stripper at the Crazy Horse Saloon,
transparent as silk stockings,
& smelling of jasmine & tea rose.

But what was that old perfume
I left in the pocket,
that cotton ball soaked
in Bal à Versailles,
that yellowing glacé glove
which lacks a mate,
that fine cambric handkerchief

brown with dried blood
from an old nosebleed?

Even poetry, pure as nothing
but snow or music,
drags life along
in its hidden pockets.

Oh for an art
that is not made of words
with all their odours
& indiscretions.

Mr Lowell

Two wives dividing him,
he died
(the third, far in the background
with her books).
He was a man who trembled much,
who drank.
He changed the landscape
of the language.

Harsh. The world is harsh
even to the wellborn,
who choke on silver spoons
& must pronounce
their vowels
a certain way;
who are born
into a family plot,
& buried at birth.

I heard him read his poems
a dozen times.
He mumbled mostly
& his hair stood up
as if with electricity. You knew
the muse had passed there often.

Real poets are as rare
as unicorns.
I don't mean girls
in capes who fall in love
with suicide;
or nasty boys in beards
who are afraid
of being influenced
by Shakespeare, Pope, or Yeats;
nor yet the critics
with their chipmunk cheeks
full of unwritten poems
better than mine . . .

No—
a real poet
is a mythological beast;
but the suffering he knows
is real.

Without Parachutes

The experiencer of fear is not
an observer of it; he is fear itself,
the very instrument of fear.
                    —J. KRISHNAMURTI

In dreams I descend
into the cave of my past:
a child with a morgue-tag
on its toe,
the terrible metal squeaking
of the morgue-drawers,
& the chilly basement
& the slam of doors . . .

Or else I am setting up dream house
with the wife
of my second ex-husband.
She complains of him
with breaking sorrow—
& I comfort her.
(She only married him, it seems, for me.)

Sometimes I wake up naked
in Beverly Hills—
the table set for ten, a formal dinner—
a studio chief on my left side,
a fabled actor on my right.
Across the table,
Greta Garbo, Scott Fitzgerald,
John F. Kennedy & Marilyn Monroe—

& I alone not properly dressed for dinner,
& besides unprepared
for the final exam,
in which our immortality
will be tested,
& one of us shall perish
as dessert.

Send parachutes & kisses!
Send them quick!
I am descending into the cave
of my own fear.
My feet are weighted
with the leg-irons of the past.
The elevator plummets
in the shaft.

Trapped, trapped in the bowels
of my dream,
locked in the cellar
by myself the jailer.
Rats and spiders scuttle
through the coal bin.
I cower in the corner.

I am fear.

Explanations

How to explain that writing a long novel
the soul changes, the soul meanders
along the bottom of a muddy river
& comes back clearer than before?

How to explain that dreams tell us
where we walked in the last life,
& will walk in the next life
& will dream in the life after that?

Accountants don't believe it; lawyers take notes
but remember nothing; scientists measure
only what is measurable
& leave out, therefore, the whole world.

How to explain that a poem, an essay, a novel,
a whole life of poems or novels
is only the tiniest tip
of the iceberg of self,

that the mystery remains
cold, dense, impenetrable
studded with bits of boulder,
precious stones, semiprecious, & those not precious at all,

until that glittering greyish mass,
that ice hippopotamus
floating through that cosmic ocean,
is melted by the heat of the pen nib

propelled by passion,
or the tip of the tongue moving over the lover,
or the eyelid floating over the dreaming sleeper
who is you & therefore who is I?

On Picking Up My
Pen Again

I am too old for poetry
that innocent flower-mama,
that butter in the muzzle of a gun.
Pull the trigger. BLAM!
A buttercup against the sun.

No poem will unwrite lawsuits,
unseat senators, or unbribe judges.
If you & I
& all the poets in the world
write poems hourly,

no cancer will ungrow.
No bullet will boomerang
& hit its maker,
& yet I know
the world is not God's fault

but ours.

We write poems
as leaves give oxygen—
so we can breathe.

If God Is a Dog

If God is a dog drowsing,
contemplating
the quintessential dogginess
of the universe, of the whole
canine race, why are we
uneasy?

No dog I know
would hurl thunderbolts,
or plant plague germs,
or shower us with darts
of pox or gonococci.
No. He lies on his back
awaiting
the cosmic belly rub;
he wags his tail signifying
universal love; he frolics and cavorts
because he has just
taken a galactic shit
& found it good.
All dogs are blessed;
they live in the now.

But God is all too human.
Somehow we have spelled his name

wrong, got it backward,
aroused his growl.
God drowses
like a lazy old man
bored
with our false
alarms.

Assuming Our Dominance

Assuming our dominance
over the creatures of earth—
dog, cat, sparrow,
tiny field mouse
(who lives in our kitchen
as a blur of light
running past the edges
of our sight)—
how can we understand humility?

The mouse-droppings
in the silverware drawer
annoy us.
The infinite insects
creep out of the walls
one by one,
only to be slammed
under our soles.
Our souls are heavy
with the deaths of animals.
Ocelot, beaver, fox
& even the ugly
slant-eyed mink
give their skins
to women

who are no more beautiful to God
than they.
The lowly roach,
or the tick
that seeks admission to our bed
on the back
of a gentle dog,
is beloved by some creator.

Assuming our dominance
has made us mad,
has made the fragrant earth
into a place
where the mice that fill the edges
of our eyes
& scuttle past our countertops
& dreams,
are fears, the lurking fears
of our own kind.

Jubilate Canis

(WITH APOLOGIES TO CHRISTOPHER SMART)

For I will consider my dog Poochkin
(& his long-lost brothers, Chekarf & Dogstoyevsky).
For he is the reincarnation of a great canine poet.
For he barks in metre, & when I leave him alone
his yelps at the door are epic.
For he is white, furry, & resembles a bathmat.
For he sleeps at my feet as I write
& therefore is my greatest critic.
For he follows me into the bathroom
& faithfully pees on paper.
For he is almost housebroken.
For he eats the dogfood I give him
but also loves Jarlsberg and Swiss cheese.
For he disdains nothing that reeks—
whether feet or roses.
For to him, all smells are created equal by God—
both turds and perfumes.
For he loves toilet bowls no less than soup bowls.
For by watching him, I have understood democracy.
For by stroking him, I have understood joy.
For he turns his belly towards God
& raises his paws & penis in supplication.
For he hangs his pink tongue out of his mouth
like a festival banner for God.
For though he is male, he has pink nipples on his belly

like the female.
For though he is canine, he is more humane
than most humans.
For when he dreams he mutters in his sleep
like any poet.
For when he wakes he yawns & stretches
& stands on his hind legs to greet me.
For, after he shits, he romps and frolics
with supreme abandon.
For, after he eats, he is more contented
than any human.
For in every room he will find the coolest corner,
& having found it, he has the sense to stay there.
For when I show him my poems,
he eats them.
For an old shoe makes him happier than a Rolls-Royce
makes a rock star.
For he has convinced me of the infinite wisdom
of dog-consciousness.
For, thanks to Poochkin, I praise the Lord
& no longer fear death.
For when my spirit flees my body through my nostrils,
may it sail into the pregnant belly
of a furry bitch,
& may I praise God always
as a dog.

Best Friends

We made them
in the image of our fears
to cry at doors,
at partings – even brief,
to beg for food at table,
& to look at us with those big
aching eyes,
& stay beside us
when our children flee,
& sleep upon our beds
on darkest nights,
& cringe at thunder
as in our own
childhood
frights.

We made them sad-eyed,
loving, loyal, scared
of life without us.
We nurtured their dependency
& grief.
We keep them as reminders of our fear.
We love them
as the unacknowledged hosts
of our own terror
of the grave – abandonment.

Hold my paw
for I am dying.
Sleep upon my coffin;
wait for me
sad-eyed
in the middle of the drive
that curves beyond the cemetery wall.

I hear your bark,
I hear your mournful howl—
oh may all dogs that I have ever loved
carry my coffin,
howl at the moonless sky,
& lie down with me sleeping
when I die.

Literature Need Not

As soon as man applies his intelligence
and only his intelligence to any object
at all, he unfailingly destroys the
object.

—TOLSTOY

Literature need not be dust
just because we fleshpeople
return to it.

The wizened grey guardians of letters
who walk
with stooped shoulders,
who inhale
the dust of libraries,
who denounce
whatever cannot be catalogued,
are no saner
than the mad young men who burn books—
only mad
in a different way.

And the matrons of letters
who disdain 'bad' language
and unlock the sanctuary of Poesy
only for a select few
are not much different really
from those who guard the restrooms.
Their keys clank too.
The temple of art is a locked restroom.
Only those with highclass bladders
may relieve themselves within.

For the rest of us—
women, blacks, third-world pissers,
Jews who refuse to be tamed—
the restroom is barred.

Ah! We will take our leaks outside—
in the open air.

Paper Stars

The little poet writes nicely
of his nice wife, his nice
kids, his nice job at the nice university,
the nice dead mice he found
on his nice snowy road,
& his nice guilt for sleeping
with his nice student.

But some are tornadoes of words,
whirling, scattering books out of the clouds—
Blake the tornado,
Whitman tornado,
Neruda the Latin tornado . . .
Words fly out of their mouths
like spittle or kisses;
their passion & anger
fill the unruly world.

& then comes the critic,
creeping along with his two pairs
of pants, & his reservations
(most of them for lunch)
& his nice distinctions,
semantic notions,

& his box full
of paper stars.

He pings one on the forehead
of the nicest poet
because no tornado
stands still
long enough.

Self-Interview

I have found that a story leaves
a deeper impression when it is
impossible to tell which side the
author is on.
                    —TOLSTOY

Which side am I on?
The side of words.
Only sometimes
I'm on the side of music—
for no one asks a chord
which side it's on.

Women?
Sometimes I like men better.
& sometimes
I'd hate to have to choose.
& sometimes
both sexes really bore me.
& sometimes
I'm on the side of dogs.

Sex?
But chastity has virtues.
Lesbos?
But Athens has its charms.
Dickens?
But Tolstoy's as engrossing.
Whitman?
But Dickinson is *terse*.

Journalists—
they always want to nail you
(as if a writer were a kind of Christ).
I see the hammer
& I open up my palms.
I have a left hand—
but I also have a right.

The Exam Dream

In a season of deaths,
when the dead ones, the great ones
were falling all around,
when the leaves were turning
scarlet, crimson, brown as blood,
when the birches trembled
& the oaks turned gold,

I dreamed,
perhaps for the last time,
the old exam-dream:
a history course
& I had not read a word.
Though I took my degree Phi Bete
with every honour,
I trembled in my dream
that I would fail.

Oh the terror
in the college corridor!
The fear of reprisals,
the fear of death.
The history of the world
is blank to me.
The only thing I know

is certain
death.

How are we tested?
Why do our minds
go blank?
Why the exam room,
courtroom,
why the witness stand?
Even the Phi Bete kids
must fail in dreams;
A's & F's are equalized
by sleep.

Perhaps we are tested by mortality.
No childhood of anxiety
& pain,
no eyes behind glasses
searching flyspeck print
can spare us
from the certain truth
we fail.

Teach us to live
each day
as if our last.
Teach us the present tense,
teach us the word.
Teach us to take air in
& let it out
without the fearful catch
of breath on death.

Truce with the cosmos,

soul at peace within,
we may stop dreaming
that we fail
life's school.

Our lives are in your hands,
our deaths assured.
Between this knowledge
& our schooldays
fall our dreams.

His Tuning of the Night

All night he lies awake tuning the sky,
tuning the night with its fat crackle of static,
with its melancholy love songs crooning
across the rainy air above Verdun
& the autobahn's blue suicidal dawn.

Wherever he lives there is the same unwomaned bed,
the ashtrays overflowing their reproaches,
his stained fingers on the tuning bar, fishing
for her voice in a deep mirrorless pond,
for the tinsel & elusive fish
(brighter than pennies in water & more wished upon)—
the copper-coloured daughter of the pond god.

He casts for her, the tuning bar his rod,
but only long-dead lovers with their griefs
haunt him in Piaf's voice—
(as if a voice could somehow only die
when it was sung out, utterly).

He finally lies down and drowns the light
but the taste of her rises, brackish,
from the long dark water of her illness
& his grief is terrible as drowning
when he reaches for the radio again.

In the daytime, you hardly know him;
he walks in a borrowed calm.
You cannot sense
his desperation in the dawn
when the abracadabras of the birds
conjure another phantom day.

He favours cities which blaze all night,
hazy mushrooms of light under the blue
& blinking eyes of jets.
But when the lamps across the way go under,
& the floorboards settle,
& the pipes fret like old men gargling—
he is alone with his mouthful of ghosts,
his tongue bitter with her unmourned death,
& the terrible drowning.

I watch from my blue window
knowing he does not trust me,
though I know him as I know my ghosts,
though I know his drowning,
though, since that night when all harmony broke for me,
I have been trying to tune the sky.

III
BLOOD & HONEY

... for out of nothing comes
nothing. But out of suffering
may come the cure. Better have
pain than paralysis.
–FLORENCE NIGHTINGALE

The Deaths of the Goddesses

It used to be hard
for women,
snowed in their white lives,
white lies,
to write books
with that fine frenzy
that commends genius
to posterity,
yet estranges it
from its closest
friends.

Women were friends to all,
& being too friendly
they could not command
the unfriendly prerogatives
of genius,
though some were
geniuses still,
destroying
only themselves
with the torment
of the unfriendly ghost
trapped in a friendly
form.

Oh the women who died
dissembling friendship
for the world!
Oh the women who turned
the dagger inward
when it wished
to go out,
who impaled themselves
on Womanhood itself!

No vampire
could be
as greedy for blood,
no father or husband
as bullying.
A woman punishing herself
with her own pain
is a fierce opponent indeed.

It is self against self,
dagger to dagger,
blood of her blood,
blood of her daughter,
blood of her mother,
her menses, her moon,
all pooled together,
one crimson sea.

It is the awful *auto de fé*,
the sublime *seppuku*,
Santa Sebastiana
as archer
& victim too.

The arrow flies from her bow.
She runs, fleet as Diana,
& stops it
with her breast.

Enough!
cried the Women-Who-Cared.
Henceforth we will turn
our anger where it belongs.
We will banish the whitest lies.
We will speak the black truth as it is.
Our fathers – we spit back their sperm.
Our husbands – we spit back their names.
Our brothers – we suck back our love.

The self-righteous inherit the earth,
& anger speaks louder than love.
Love is a softness
the weak cannot afford,
& sex a Darwinian bribe.

But who wants the earth as a gift
when it is empty as space,
when women grow hard
as bronze madonnas
& Diana loves only her stag?

When Persephone stays in hell
the entire year,
then how can spring
begin?

The Truce Between
the Sexes

For a long time unhappy
with my man,
I blamed men,
blamed marriage, blamed
the whole bleeding world,
because I could not lie in bed with him
without lying to him
or else to myself
& lying to myself
became increasingly hard
as my poems
struck rock.

My life & my poems lived apart;
I had to marry them,
& marrying them
meant divorcing him,
divorcing the lie.

Now I lie in bed
with my poems on the sheets
& a man I love
sleeping or reading
at my side.

Because I love him,
I do not think of him
as 'Men',
but as my friend.
Hate generalizes;
love is particular.

He is not Men, man, male—
all those maddening m's
muttering like machine-gun spittle,
but only a person like me,
dreaming, vulnerable, scared,
his dreams
opening into rooms
where the chairs
are wishes you can sit on
& the rugs are wonderful
with oriental birds.

The first month we lived together
I was mad with joy,
thinking that a person with a penis
could dream, tell jokes, even cry . . .
Now I find it usual,
& when other women sputter
of their rage,
I look at them blankly,
half comprehending
those poor medieval creatures
from a dark, dark age.

I wonder about myself.
Was I always so fickle?
Must politics always be personal?

If I struck oil,
would I crusade
for depletion allowances?

Erica, Erica,
you are hard on yourself.
Lie back & enjoy the cease-fire.
Trouble will come again.
Sex will grow horns & warts.
The white sheets of this bed
will be splattered with blood.
Just wait.

But I don't believe it.
There will be trouble enough,
but a different sort.

Inner Dialogue

I know men—
the wars gathering like storms,
the blood rising up for blood,
the pounding in the heart that says:
I'd rather win than live.

I know death—
his bloodless womb gives birth to men,
his lightless moon shines on their birth.
He knows them like an evil father
who plans to eat his sons.

I know myself—
the rages, the envies and hates
that inhabit my smiling face.
I love so few – yet no one better than myself
& yet myself not well.

I know hope—
it is in spite of all
I know of men or death or me.

Depression in Early Spring

Meathooks, notebooks,
the whole city sky palely flaming
& spectral bombs
hitting that patch of river
I see from my eastern window.

The poets are dead, the city dying.
Anne, Sylvia, Keats
with his passionate lungs,
Berryman jumping from the bridge & waving,
all the dreamers dead
of their own dreams.

Why have I stayed on as Horatio?
Anne sends poems from the grave,
Sylvia, letters.
John Keats' ghostly cough
comes through the wallboard.
What am I doing here?
Why contend?

I am a corpse who moves a pen that writes.
I am a vessel for a voice that echoes.
I write a novel & annihilate whole forests.
I rearrange the cosmos by an inch.

Pornflicks

Who wants to see
other lovers
doing it?

Not me.
What skin does to skin
is not capturable
by camera.

Bright or obscure,
eight or sixteen millimetre,
nothing gives
the silken feel
of sex,
but sex.

One touch
is worth a thousand pictures.

But they will go on
selling it—
the way medieval hucksters
sold pieces
of 'the true cross',
or 'pigges bones'

for holy saints'
drumsticks.

Chaucer was right
about everything.
Those who can't tell
the difference
deserve to be fucked
with their eyes open.

Blood & Honey

I began by loving women
& the love turned
to bitterness.

My mother, the bitter,
whose bitter lesson—
trust no one,
especially no one male—
caused me to be naïve
for too many years,
in mere rebellion
against that bitterness.

If she was Medea,
I would be Candide
& bleed in every sexual war,
& water my garden in menstrual blood
& grow the juiciest fruits.

(Like the woman
who watered her roses with blood
& won all the prizes,
though no one knew why.)

If she was Lady Macbeth,

I would be Don Quixote—
& never pass up a windmill
without a fight,
& never choose discretion
over valour.

My valour was often foolish.
I was rash
(though others called me brave).
My poems were red flags
To lure the bulls.
The picadors smelled blood
& jabbed my novels.

I had only begun
by loving women—
& ended by hating their deceit,
hating the hate
they feed their daughters,
hating the self-hate
they feed themselves,
hating the contempt
they feed their men,
as they claim weakness—
their secret strength.

For who can be crueller
than a woman
who is cruel
out of her impotence?
& who can be meaner
than a woman
who desires
the only room with a view?

Even in chess
she shouts:
'Off with their heads!'
& the poor king
walks one step forward,
one step back.

But I began
by loving women,
loving myself
despite my mother's lesson,
loving my ten fingers,
ten toes, my puckered navel,
my lips that are too thick
& my eyes the colour of ink.

Because I believed in them,
I found gentle men.
Because I loved myself,
I was loved.
Because I had faith,
the unicorn licked my arm,
the rabbit nestled in my skirts,
the griffin slept
curled up at the bottom
of my bed.

Bitter women,
there is milk under this poem.
What you sow in blood
shall be harvested in honey.

Woman Enough

Because my grandmother's hours
were apple cakes baking,
& dust motes gathering,
& linens yellowing
& seams and hems
inevitably unravelling—
I almost never keep house—
though really I *like* houses
& wish I had a clean one.

Because my mother's minutes
were sucked into the roar
of the vacuum cleaner,
because she waltzed with the washer-dryer
& tore her hair waiting for repairmen—
I send out my laundry,
& live in a dusty house,
though really I *like* clean houses
as well as anyone.

I am woman enough
to love the kneading of bread
as much as the feel
of typewriter keys
under my fingers—

springy, springy.
& the smell of clean laundry
& simmering soup
are almost as dear to me
as the smell of paper and ink.

I wish there were not a choice;
I wish I could be two women.
I wish the days could be longer.
But they are short.
So I write while
the dust piles up.

I sit at my typewriter
remembering my grandmother
& all my mothers,
& the minutes they lost
loving houses better than themselves—
& the man I love cleans up the kitchen
grumbling only a little
because he knows
that after all these centuries
it is easier for him
than for me.

I Must Have Done Something

I must have done something amazing
in my last life,
something wonderful,
something I do not remember
–because they sent me you
in this life—

you with your tigery eyes
& your strawberry mouth
with your funny beard,
& your cosmic cuddles
& your fuzzy stomach
& your solar plexus
glowing like a sun
against mine.

I must have done something astounding—
won a holy war
built a great cathedral,
carved a marble statue of the pope
which was a perfect likeness
(flattering yet true)
because they sent me you.

I must have saved a species from extinction,

invented penicillin, radar, soap,
or maybe even marbles,
chocolate mousse, celery tonic,
washable latex paint . . .
I must have been a saint.

IV
HOUSE-
HUNTING

People wish to be settled;
only as far as they are unsettled
is there any hope for them.
—RALPH WALDO EMERSON

House-Hunting, 1976

Looking for a home, America,
we have split & crisscrossed
you from your purple seashores
to your nongrip, nonslip
motel bathrooms,
from the casinos at Reno
to the crystalline shores of Lake Tahoe,
from the giant duck in Southampton
(which is really an egg shop)
to the giant hotdog in L.A.
(which is really a hotdog stand)
to the giant artichoke in Castroville, CA,
the heart of the artichoke
country,
& still we are homeless
this 1976.

America,
we have met your brokers.
They are fiftyish ladies in hairnets,
or fiftyish ladies in blue & silver hair like mink coats
or flirty fiftyish ladies
getting blonder every winter.
They tout your federal brickwork
& your random hand-pegged floorboards.

Like witches, they advertise your gingerbread houses,
your 'high ranches', your split-levels,
your Victorians, your widows' walks,
your whaling towns,
instead of wailing walls,
your Yankee New England spunk,
your hospitality, your tax rates,
your school systems,
with or without busing,
your friendly dogs
& philosophical cats.

America,
we have ridden through your canyons,
passes, dried-up rivers,
past your flooded quarries, through your eroded arroyos.
We have sighted UFOs on the beach
at Malibu
& swum from pool to pool
like any Cheever hero
& lusted in motels like any Updike Christian.

America,
the open road is closing,
a tollbooth blocks the vista,
& even the toilets are pumped
with dimes as well as shit.
The fried clams on Cape Cod
are pressed from clam scraps.
The California carrot cake is rumoured
to be made of soy.

The dreaming towers of Gotham
are sunk in garbage,

the bedrock softens,
the buildings list like drunks,
the Thanksgiving balloons are all deflated,
the Christmas trees don't even pretend to be green.
But we love you, America,
& we'll keep on hunting.
The dream house that we seek is just next door.
Switzerland is a heaven of chocolates
& tax breaks.
Barbados is sweet & black & tax-free.
Antigua is Britain by the sea.

But we're sticking around, America,
for the next earthquake,
kissing the ground
for the next Fourth of July.
We love you, America,
& we'll keep hunting.

There's a dream house waiting for us somewhere
with blooming cherry trees
& a FOR SALE sign,
with picture windows facing the Pacific
& dormer windows facing the Atlantic,
with coconut palms & flaming maples,
with shifting sand dunes
& canyons blazing with mustard,
with rabbits & rattlesnakes & nonpoisonous scorpions,
with raccoons who rattle the garbage
& meekly feeding deer who lap at salt licks
& pheasants who hop across the lawn in two-steps,
with loving dogs & aloof, contemplative cats,
with heated swimming pool & sauna
& an earthquake-proof Jacuzzi,

with carpeted carport & bathrooms
& plumbing so good it hums,
with neighbours who lend you organic sugar
& mailmen who are often women,
with huge supermarkets selling wine & kneesocks,
mangoes, papayas, & dogfood in fifty flavours,
with nearby movie theatres playing Bergman & Fellini
without dubbing,
with resident symphony orchestras
down the block,
but no rock stars living right next door.

We know we'll find you someday
if not in this life, America,
then in the next,
if not in this solar system,
then in another.
We're ready to move, America.
We've called our unscrupulous Mafia movers
who always break everything & demand to be paid in
cash,
& we have our downpayment in hand.
We lust for a big fat mortgage.
We've pulled up our city roots
& we've packed our books, our banjo & our dog
in a bright red gypsy wagon
with low gas mileage.

All we need is the house,
all we need is the listing.
We're ready to move, America,
but we don't know
where.

January in New York

. . . the night travels in its black ship . . .
                                     –PABLO NERUDA

Black ship of night
sailing through the world
& the moon an orange slice
tangy to the teeth
of lovers who lie
under it,
sucking it.

Somewhere there are palm trees;
somewhere the sea
bluely gathers itself up
& lets itself fall again
into green;
somewhere the spangles
of light on the ocean
dazzle the eyes;
but here in the midnight city,
the black ship of night
has docked
for a long, dark stay,
& even the citrus moon
with its pockets of juice
cannot sweeten the dark.

Then the snow begins,

whirling over the Pole,
gathering force over Canada,
sprinkling the Great Lakes with sugar
which drowns in their deep black cups;
it is drawn to the spires of New York
& the flurries come
scampering at first,
lighthearted, crystalline, white,
but finally
sucked into the city
as into a black hole
in space.

The sky is suddenly pink—
pink as flesh: breasts,
babies' bottoms. Night is
day; day is whiter than the desert;
the city stops like a heart;
pigeons dip & veer
& come to rest
under the snow-hatted
watertanks.

New England Winter

Testing the soul's mettle,
the frost heaves
holes in the roads
to the heart,
the glass forest
raises up its branches
to praise all things
that catch the light
then melt.
The forest floor is white,
but here & there a boulder rises
with its glacial arrogance
& brooks that bubble
under sheets of ice
remind us that the tundra of the soul
will soften
just a little
towards the spring.

UFO Poem

(or, the grass is always greener on the other side
of the galaxy)

The little men arrive upon the beach
marching like mushrooms
with immobile feet,
invading our dreams,
dreaming our beaches,
teaching us
with their gentle, mocking ways
not to mock the stars.

Moons away,
we dream of landing
on a planet
pink as new pennies,
with clouds the colour of bubblegum
& lakes bubbling
with strawberry bath-foam.

Through crystal telescopes,
the green inhabitants observe
that we are pink,
the colour of their planet.

'Tiny pinkies',
they call us
in their curious, gurgly language,

marvelling that our skins
should be the colour
of their earth,
that our eyes
should be the colours
of our trees, our skies.

They dream of landing
on our lovely planet,
of rolling greenly
on our green lawns,
bathing bluely
in our blue waters,
skipping blithely through the air
of our pale beaches
like little Frisbees,
flying saucers,
magic mushrooms,
wishes, wishes . . .

We are their wishes
& surely
they are

ours.

Westering

Brainless California,
the hills
humping brownly down
to the azure sea,
the bougainvillea going mad
in purple
& cactuses inheriting
the earth.

I leave the tired, grey spires
of New York,
arrogant on so much bedrock—
as if no tower
could sink a city,
no earth reverse
its upward thrust.

I leave Westchester
dreaming drably
of merry England,
Fire Island playing
pirate beach,
& flying west across
the continental span,
my heart lifts

with the old westward dream . . .
I feel my eyes widen
in the West.

Europe is old stones,
old plots,
new parties
promising colour TVs
in every pot,
& pink tile bidets
for liberated
women—

but out here in the West
no one is dirty,
& the sun is too brilliant
to stay indoors.

When the UFOs land on the beach,
we'll be ready.
When the pale hairless men
& their transparent women
beckon us to rise,
we'll follow.

Here in the West,
everything happens.

Today, California,
tomorrow,
the stars.

I Live in New York

I am happiest
near the ocean,
where the changing light
reminds me of my death
& the fact that it need not be fatal—

yet I perch here
in the midst of the city
where the traffic dulls my senses,
where my ears scream at sirens,
where transistor radio blasts
invade my poems
like alien war chants.

But I never walk
the streets of New York
without hoping for the end
of the world.

How many years
before the streets return to flowers?
How many centuries
before the towers fall?

In my mind's eye,

New York falls to ruins.
Butterflies alight upon the stones
and poppies spring
out of the asphalt fields.

Why do I stay here
when I love the ocean?
Because the ocean lulls me
with its peace.
Eternity is coming soon enough.
As monks sleep
in their own coffins,

I live in New York.

Flight to Catalina

On a darkening planet
speeding
towards our death,
we pierce a rosy cloud
& hit clean air,
we glide above
the red infernal smog,
we leave the mammon city
far behind.

Here – where the air is clear
as nothing,
where cactus pads
are prickly as stars,
where buffalo chips
are gilded by the sun,
& the moon tastes like a peppermint—
we land.

'Have we flown to heaven?'
I inquired
(& I meant it).
The airport was a levelled
mountaintop.
We took the cloudbank

at a tilt
& bumped the runway
just ten degrees from crashing,
certain death.

If I'm to die, God,
let me die flying!
Fear is worse than death—
I know that now.
The cloudbanks of my life
have silver linings.
Beyond them:
cactus pads,
clear earth,
dear sky.

Good Carpenters

I mourn a dead friend, like
myself, a good carpenter.
 —PABLO NERUDA ABOUT
  CÉSAR VALLEJO

I looked at the book.
'It will stand,' I thought.
Not a palace
built by a newspaper tsar,
nor a mud hovel
that the sea will soften,
but a good house of words
near the sea
with everything plumb.
That is the most I can ask.

I have cut the wood myself
from my own forests,
I have sanded it smooth
with the grain.
I have left knotholes
for the muse to whistle through
– old siren that she is.

At least the roof does not leak.
& the fireplace is small
but it draws.
The wind whips the house
but it stands.
& the waves lick

the pilings with their tongues
but at least they do not suck me
out to sea.
The sea is wordless
but it tries to talk to us.
We carpenters are also translators.
We build with sounds, with whispers, & with wind.
We try to speak the language of the sea.

We want to build to last
yet change forever.
We want to be as endless as the sea.
& yet she mocks us
with her barnacles & rust-stains;
she tells us what we build will also fall.

Our words are grains of sand,
our walls are wood,
our windowpanes are sprayed with solemn salt.
We whisper, as we build, 'Forever please',
– by which we mean at least for thirty years.

People Who Live

People who live by the sea
understand eternity.
They copy the curves of the waves,
their hearts beat with the tides,
& the saltiness of their blood
corresponds with the sea.

They know that the house of flesh
is only a sandcastle
built on the shore,
that skin breaks
under the waves
like sand under the soles
of the first walker on the beach
when the tide recedes.

Each of us walks there once,
watching the bubbles
rise up through the sand
like ascending souls,
tracing the line of the foam,
drawing our index fingers
along the horizon,
pointing home.

Unrequited

Parachuting
down through clouds
shaped like whales & sharks,
dolphins & penguins,
pelicans & gulls,
we reach
the purple hills
of a green-hearted island
ringed
with volcanic rock
bathed
by cobalt waters
reefed
by whitest coral
tenanted
by sea urchins & sponge
& visited
by barracuda
& tourists.

The dictator
of this island
is the sun.

The Secret Police
is the sweet
fragrance of cane.
Frangipani grows
in the uplands;
the salt flats
reek
by the sea.

I want to buy it,
to hide here,
to stay,
to teach all the people
to write,
to orchestrate the stars
in the palm trees
& teach the jellyfish
not to bite.

Oh dark volcanic
wine!
Oh collapsed parachute
filled with kisses!
Oh blue-bottle bits
ground
into jewels
by the sand!

Whoever loves islands
must love the sea,
& the sea
loves no one
but herself.

Summoning the Muse to a New House

Woodsprites
& deer arrive;
raccoons hitch a night ride
in the still car
& eat all the Life Savers
from the glove compartment;
woodchucks feast
on the vegetable seedlings;
a swarm of honeybees
breaks loose from a neighbouring hive
& storms my third-floor
study window
in search of honey;
a bitch in heat
seeks out
our horny dog;
a hawk nests
in the fir tree
outside my window;
spiders weave
& spin their webs
from book to book,
from typewriter to ceiling beam;
but still the muse—
recalcitrant & slow—
does not arrive.

Her skirts snag
on the Rocky Mountains,
her blue hair trails
into the Pacific.
'You move too often,'
she accuses;
'I just get acclimated,
then you move again!'

Bitter muse,
you ought to be portable
as a typewriter.
You ought to be
transient as a spy,
adaptable as a diplomat,
self-effacing as the perfect
valet—
but you are not.

After all,
you are our mother;
unless we listen & obey,
you let us starve.

Come – there is honey here,
or at least, bees.
The honey's
in the making . . .
if you come.

About the Author

Erica Jong is the author of three previous books of poetry: *Fruits & Vegetables* (1971), *Half-Lives* (1973), and *Loveroot* (1975). She has also published internationally acclaimed novels, *Fear of Flying* (1973), *How to Save Your Own Life* (1977)

Erica Jong's poetry has been awarded numerous prizes. It has been translated into Swedish, Danish, Italian, German, French, Spanish, and Japanese, while her novels have appeared in more than twenty-five foreign editions.